I Am NOT a Parrot

a Parrot

ANIMALS IN THE RAIN FOREST

BY MARI BOLTE

PEBBLE
a capstone imprint

Published by Pebble, an imprint of Capstone
1710 Roe Crest Drive, North Mankato, Minnesota 56003
capstonepub.com

Library of Congress Cataloging-in-Publication Data
Names: Bolte, Mari, author. Title: I am not a parrot : animals in the rain forest / by Mari Bolte.
Description: North Mankato, Minnesota : Pebble, [2022] | Series: What animal am I? | Audience: Ages 5-8 | Audience: Grades K-1 | Summary: "The rain forest is a hot, wet place with many kinds of animals. It is my home. I make a lot of sounds but am not a parrot. I sleep a lot but am not a sloth. Can you guess which animal I am by reading the clues in the book?"— Provided by publisher.
Identifiers: LCCN 2021050685 (print) | LCCN 2021050686 (ebook) | ISBN 9781666343410 (hardcover) | ISBN 9781666343458 (paperback) | ISBN 9781666343496 (pdf) | ISBN 9781666343571 (kindle edition) Subjects: LCSH: Mountain gorilla—Juvenile literature. | Rain forest animals—Juvenile literature. Classification: LCC QL737.P94 B65 2022 (print) | LCC QL737.P94 (ebook) | DDC 599.884—dc23/eng/20211124
LC record available at https://lccn.loc.gov/2021050685
LC ebook record available at https://lccn.loc.gov/2021050686

Editorial Credits
Editor: Christianne Jones; Designer: Bobbie Nuytten; Media Researcher: Morgan Walters; Production Specialist: Polly Fisher

Image Credits
Shutterstock: Attila JANDI, 30Bottom of Form, Braian Moreno, 14, top left 27, davemhuntphotography, 6, top right 26, dptro, 10, middle left 26, Jiri Hrebicek, 18, middle left 27, John And Penny, 8, bottom middle 26, Lauren Bilboe, 22, bottom left 27, Lukas Kovarik, 20, middle right 27, Nick Fox, (inset parrot) Cover, Onyx9, 28, Ruben Suria Photography, 24, bottom right 27, SaveJungle, (forest) design element, ShutterOK, 12, middle right 26, Taras Vyshnya, 2, Teo Tarras, (background) Cover, terekhov igor, 4, top left 26, Vaclav Sebek, 16, top right 27

Who Am I?

The rain forest is a hot, wet place with many kinds of animals. Tall, green trees fill the land. It is where I live.

But what animal am I? Read the clues to find out!

I am social and live in a group. When it is time to rest I go to my nest. I am known for the many sounds I can make.

But I am not a parrot.

The trees in the rain forest are my home. I use my feet to climb and hold on to branches and leaves. My good eyesight helps me find food.

But I am not a tree frog.

I am very strong. Lifting things many times my own weight is easy. Males of my species are larger than females.

But I am not a rhinoceros beetle.

I have a mouth full of sharp teeth! Powerful jaws give me a strong bite. Big, pointy canine teeth make me look scary.

But I am not a tiger.

I am huge! I can weigh more than 400 pounds (180 kilograms). My coloring helps me blend into my surroundings.

But I am not an anaconda.

Yum! I think insects are delicious! When I move, I use the back of my hand. This is called knuckle walking.

But I am not an anteater.

I have only one baby at a time. Both males and females help care for babies. Babies stay with their parents for a long time.

But I am not a king vulture.

I mark my territory with strong smells. This tells other animals to keep out! I am not seen in the wild very often.

But I am not an okapi.

Zzzzzzz. I like to sleep a lot. When I wake up I can be found climbing through the trees.

But I am not a sloth.

I am a mammal. I am also a primate. My eyes face forward. This means that I can easily see how close or far away things are.

But I am not a lemur.

I am part of the great ape family. My large body is covered in hair. I like to eat fruit in trees.

But I am not an orangutan.

I am not a parrot

or a tree frog

or a tiger

or an anaconda

or a beetle

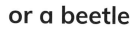

or a vulture

or an anteater

or a sloth

or an okapi

or a lemur

or an orangutan.

So what animal am I?

I am a mountain gorilla!

I can climb trees like many animals, but I spend most of the day on the ground. I eat fruit, vegetables, and bugs. I live in family groups called troops.

COOL FACTS ABOUT GORILLAS

Gorillas are part of the great ape family. Orangutans, gibbons, bonobos, chimpanzees, and humans are also great apes.

Up to 30 gorillas live together in a troop. They are led by one strong adult male.

There are only about 1,000 mountain gorillas left on Earth.

Gorillas are very smart. They have learned how to use sign language to talk to people.

There are four species of gorilla: mountain, Cross River, western lowland, and eastern lowland. All four species are in danger of dying out.

Human germs can make gorillas sick. It is important that humans do not pass on illnesses like the common cold or COVID-19.

Books in This Series

Author Bio

Mari Bolte is an author and editor of children's books on all sorts of subjects, from graphic novels about science to art projects to hands-on history. She lives in southern Minnesota in the middle of a forest full of animals.